AND

Offering 10 From
Award-Winning Journalist & Poet
Mary Michelle Jefferson ***aka***
Dr. Mylia Tiye Mal Jaza

A Call To All To Accept
The Power Of Human Choice And
Wield It Skillfully In The Fight For Life

AND

Written/Edited/Illustrated By

Mylia Tiye Mal Jaza

AND

ISBN: 978-0-557-97318-7

Author
Mylia Tiye Mal Jaza
myliajaza.gqnu.net
mylia@bepublished.biz

Self-Publishing Associate
BePublished.Org
Chicago, IL
mari@bepublished.org

Dr. Mary M. Jefferson
P.O. Box 8324
Jackson, MS 39284

Publisher of Record
Lulu Enterprises, Inc.
860 Aviation Parkway, Suite 300
Morrisville, NC 27560

First Edition
Printed in the United States of America.
Recycled Paper Encouraged.

TABLE OF CONTENTS

<u>Biography</u>

<u>Essays</u>

Life Keeps Cracking The Whip

Understanding that it is impossible to live a life that is free of hardship and heartache is difficult for me to accept. What I can stand under is the security I find in believing that, no matter what conundrums I face, I'll be okay ultimately because Jah (God) and I got me covered. I'll try hard not to complain.

No matter what, I'm confident that I'll decide to do or not do something that will make today's complications be distant experiences or forgotten memories tomorrow. I'm not saying I am the ultimate *problem solver*, but I am offering my notion that an introspection which considers the fractured self can be a *problem evolver*. This is especially true when we look at moments when a person may feel whipped by life's objectives, traumas, and achievements.

There are all kinds of objectives that life outlines for us – some we learn about earlier in life, and others are assigned to us later. As infants, one objective we had was to communicate our basic needs so they could be met. Some babies have this goal so mastered to where their mothers can "tell by the cry" what the current need is. As growing kids, we had to learn to show respect and properly complete household chores and schoolwork, among other things.

When we became teens, our goals for school, activities, organizations, first jobs, home life and social life almost-simultaneously abound as we work to solidify our character in preparation for adulthood. Once well into that coveted life of adult freedom, our objectives include completing items on a seemingly endless list of "must," "want," "need," and "have to." To do, or to have done, any of these things during any stage, we first looked within to assess our own capability and willingness.

Based on the ending result, we celebrated success or lamented losses. Some losses, some failures, hurt way more than others or flat out traumatize you more when you think about some of the bad things that can suddenly happen or has already taken place.

There have been some people who have chosen to cide-out (resort to forms of suicide and murder) while other people have chosen to plan their way out of being buried under chunks of shattered joy. The difference is not the courage to face being whipped down physically, mentally, emotionally and spiritually. It is the courage to actively resume or start anew.

I know people say some folks are afraid of their own success, but I don't personally know anyone who does not want to succeed or who fears paydays and financial security. But what I have seen are occasions when success was overshadowed or celebrations were rattled. There have been people saddened by being awarded something they felt another person deserved, along with those who got bad news shortly before or after performing / competing / testing, etc. Maybe this is why the old folks would say, "Joy is a precious thang."

I know my life has been no ice cream social, and that as beautiful as it is, it is also cruel at times. Still, I maintain that it matters not the troubles of life find us at any time. What matters is what we choose to do (or not do) about each matter at hand.

Some people seek the counsel of loved ones or colleagues when life cracks the whip on their backs, while others seek counsel from clergy or writings of their religion. Then, there's that group who would agree with my notion that such times are plum ripe for introspection.

Don't misunderstand me, do what you feel you must – just also make time for you (with or without pen and paper) and ask yourself questions like: "How do I really feel?" "Why?" and "What can I do to move forward?"

Disliked Then Ignored

Some things I believe may be in line with some things you believe. Other utterings will be concepts you are not willing to embrace. Yet, this message is not given to challenge anyone's religious or spiritual beliefs. It exists to express my own. In general, I believe we are all spiritual beings who are the strongest souls.

I also believe we were put on Earth to solve the problems in, and of, it while honoring Our Creator and enjoying each other as much as possible. But in every religion, there are people who think it's okay to ignore those who have supported them because they are not as positive or fun as they usually are. This can be proven easily by noting a few recent reactions to things said/done/not.

At a point when I was processing five deaths that occurred over a four- to six-week period (not in 2008 but 2010), I learned that people are willing to listen to you as long as you are saying the same type of nothingness that they've been hearing and want to hear. But if you are venting about your own situation to say things you need to say for yourself, they do not want to hear it.

These are the same people who seem like they always have a listening ear for you and me. Well, I quickly realized that their ears only work when we're saying *certain catchy* things but don't when we're saying *curtain snatching* things. This is why, when people say what needs to be said to express a real feeling, others say, "you're wrong" and "you're in an ugly place."

No matter how much my life may suck during any particular moment – or how bad it may sound for me to say I do not expect God to come to my rescue – I do not linger in "wrong . . . ugly" places because my life is beautiful overall. But I could have returned to my beautiful life from the ugly place a lot quicker had I not been given the added distraction of the death of a new friendship.

I'm sure, her perspective is that it was not a matter of a willingness to listen or disliking what was being said, but it was more about what was done. Her tone definitely would have made any third-party listener think that I had just arrived at a crowded event, pulled a Kanye West and snatched someone's microphone, then drank blood as I proclaimed myself a mixture of Mary and Jesus.

Even before getting off the phone, she reminded, "Who do you think it is that enables you to do anything you do? You can't do nothing without God." I concurred wholeheartedly. So all I said in response to that particular part of her outro was, "Yep, that's right."

To no surprise to those who have known me for years, I didn't try to explain myself again. I have since made it a practice to cease attempts to ever explain the obvious to the dumb or correct a belief of the erroneously convinced. I'm too impatient for that.

Some people reading what I've written here may say the problem boils down to something neither the friend-demoted-to-associate nor I did. Maybe we didn't say something or didn't say the right things. Maybe we didn't do something, or didn't do the right things.

There is validity to that as well. I had attended a memorial with her because her younger sister, who had adult children, had died. I was also dealing with $2,000 worth of expenses, where half of it arose suddenly over two days and all four of my bank accounts put together would not cover it. Maybe these elements contributed to our being unable to understand each other.

Words matter because of their vibrations, and actions matter because of their visualizations. Even choosing to not speak or act is still a communication. The value of seeing eyes and listening ears is determined by the weight of words and actions. Likewise, the value of words and actions is determined by the readiness of eyes and ears.

You probably have a similar story. If so, I think it is safe for me to say that we agree that combating limited scopes goes beyond giving back what's been imparted. It is also about being the loving support that is needed at the time. Let's try to not repeat these actions. Let's not forget the importance of not ignoring a person because they said/did/not something we didn't like.

Where's The Reciprocity

I used to get a lot of whippings when I was kid. Momma used a belt, a switch she'd send me to get, or even her green house shoe to get me to acquiesce to the ideas that I am to "turn the other cheek" and "treat people like I want to be treated" no matter how terribly they've just treated me.

The Golden Rule seemed pretty rusty to me. I once, or a hundred times, got slapped in the mouth for saying, "I do unto others as they do to me" and "I'm treating them the way they treated me like they wanted."

Today, I still think the same way, and I've deduced that only those adults who seek to use or mistreat other adults wished any grown person thought as my mother tried to raise me to think. True, she did it because it was the Christian way of child rearing (Bible based). However, when traversing paths of life, it was quickly confirmed for me that there is no benefit to me if I am suffering at the hands of another.

Life shows any person looking how there are more people who would rather stick to playing villain or victim roles than there are beings willing to stop receiving whatever and start depositing positivity into another person's life (or even their own). So since we keep hearing it is better to give than to receive, and what we put out is what we get, I propose people begin making life better by recognizing, analyzing and disseminating more reciprocity in all their relationships.

By recognizing, first, that reciprocity is simply getting what you've given, anyone can see that it is something already valued by a number of people known of or known personally. Reciprocating responsibility and goodwill are among those unspoken expectations that underline most human interactions – especially in areas like the home, business and roadways.

When we recognize the need to deposit and accept these good things (even in love or friendship), a person can see what s/he has given in the past, what is presently required, and what can be offered in the future in an effort to maintain a healthy relationship or form a mutually-beneficial association. Recognizing reciprocity eliminates unethical employment situations, worn-down spouses, or former friends still denying why they've been kicked to the curb or excommunicated to Cleveland.

Analysis of life's reciprocals takes recognition a step farther in preparation for the action phase. Analysis affords one the ability to review interactions while simultaneously seeking areas where needs were met or improvements should be implemented. Best of all, completed analysis outlines a resource that can be consciously or unconsciously referenced in any situation. Some people call it their gut, or mind, or heart that helps them know what is what.

Whatever it is, it is this thing analyzing data then sending a message about it to let you know the unknown, or to show you the unseen. This is why the ability to comprehend and decipher verbal and nonverbal information is key to successful relationships. Analysis of varying degrees of reciprocity is our strategy to determine if people are receiving the genuine affection they've given or if they're just getting *surface feeds* (those expressions/actions of a person's ego aimed at getting beneficial reactions from the listener/receiver).

Once a person knows the role reciprocity plays in life, it is up to that person to spreading it. It is up to each of us whether we disseminate the wealth found within this rule of human engagement today or tomorrow – but we must share it.

Whether you discuss the principal with colleagues during a casual conversation, or with family and friends when a situation demands that the lack of it is addressed, is totally up to you. People need to know that you have a standard for living that does not accommodate you "steppin'-n-fetchin'" or being anyone's diaper (unless that person is your "do boy" or "do girl" and is all over your butt to gladly take your mess).

I'll say it like this: If real recognizes real, then fraudulence cannot hide among authenticity. Thus, those who give a certain something of themselves should not help but notice and adjust when nothing of the kind is being bestowed unto them. Now, if what my mother and others believe works better for you, stick to it. But if it doesn't, employ my advice and require reciprocity.

I know that not everybody has had their fill of things like being abused or made an afterthought, but I am not the only one who's sick of not seeing reciprocity and wondering if Carmen San Diego stole it. It is for those who work hard and do right but are rarely properly rewarded that reciprocity is needed. Moreover, it is needed by us all to assure the love source that drives us never dries up or needs to temporarily close for repairs.

Climbing Hills With Broken Arms

Imagining someone maimed while climbing a hill while at war, we imagine a display of survival's will.

We find relativity in it because we are also seeing ourselves struggle to stay alive as we fight a different kind of war. Watching war movies give us a good glimpse of what our spiritual struggle to "stay positive and try again" looks like. Recalling life's tragedies and travesties, one can become perplexed at how people can literally climb hills when their actual limbs are damaged.

We know that action, prayer and faith can work. So we should also know that anyone *could* overcome obstacles when their usual resources are depleted. And, we should know we can climb hills (make it through hardship) despite a broken leg or a broken arm (trauma to our soul and body). Overcoming stumbling blocks and maintaining joy are handled in pretty much the same way as scaling mounds despite being cast bound, with: (1) planning, (2) persistence, and (3) pain.

Planning out courses of action create a ladder to a goal. Anytime a limitation exists, a person can utilize another mean/option. Focusing just on the arms, if both are broken, the person can plan to walk up the hill while keeping steepness and balance in mind. If finding a job is the goal and the broken limbs are no responses to emailed resumes and no money to buy newspapers or internet access to see who's hiring, then get a library card and go to the library once a week to use the internet to search for jobs. When emailing your resume, instead of just attaching it as a document, also include it as text in the email to boost its chance of being read.

Being persistent, refusing to give-up, is another way to assure an objective will be achieved despite time required or assistance lacking. Hanging in there no matter what happens is not as easily done as it is frequently suggested. But endurance can be achieved when motivation is continually or periodically replenished. Another way to become and remain persistent is to stay focused on life after the goal is achieved, which helps us not let the disappointment of failure and bad experiences derail us.

Pain can run so deeply that it is able to be cathartic for those seeking situational improvements. Getting past the pain of yesterday, and enduring the pain of today, helps us to avert future's pain every time we have the chance to do so. In doing so though, we must accept that there is no way to have a life that is completely pain-free. Since pain is ever present or possible, we have to vow to not allow it to stop us from putting measures in place to extinguish it at will.

As you can see, it doesn't matter if you are speaking figuratively or literally about moving forward while wounded, because the solutions are the same for scaling mounds despite being cast bound. Anytime an arm/leg is broken, a person can still climb with the other arm/leg with planning. Focusing just on the arms, if both are broken, the person can plan to just walk up the hill with only steepness and balance presenting a challenge above pain.

A person who must climb to have a chance at survival will find a way to attempt to scale what s/he must, even with both arms broken at the shoulder. If nothing else proves this, it should be proven just by looking at the fact that most people go to work out of payday planning instead of volunteering.

I used to think that all it took to get through hard times was a bit of action, prayer and faith. Then there were periods when I wondered why that didn't seem to be enough because prayers were unanswered, but even that was overcome. I've since learned that no matter what we are going through, we can always try to solve it by the methods that seem best at the time, and by accepting a little planning, persistence, and pain. There is nothing we can experience that will take away "us" from us. We can always bounce back despite traumas to our souls and bodies.

Best Things In Life Life Are Pricey

All my life, I've heard that "the best things in life are free." That's not factual and is just more feel-good propaganda like, "what you don't know won't hurt you" and "you take one step, God will take two." Ignorance kills; and everything that I've ever needed done didn't get done until I did it (or it isn't done yet, despite faith and prayers).

Among the best things we have in life are the basic necessities – water, food, shelter, clothing, education and affection. None of these things are nowhere near free.

Then when we consider the luxurious things offered in today's world – uber-pregnant bank accounts, private yachts and jets, personal assistants/chefs and housekeeping staff, high-end automobiles, and mega mansions – we definitely know the best things in life are pricey.

Food and water aren't free, although we all know it's best to eat so you won't starve to death. Shelter and clothing are not free, although we know we all need protection from the climatic elements outside our homes. Education and affection aren't free either, although we all need these and need to share these just to be able to function at our optimal levels in every aspect of our own lives.

Looking closely at food and water alone, anyone can argue they should be made available for free to every person in the world. These are two things that we know the lack of will quickly kill us. If a person can't grow their own food and haul water from a spring or a river, he or she will have to barter or buy food and water from someone.

The thing is, while food and water are readily available around the world, the means of acquisition may be too great for the person in need to easily or ever meet.

Many people living in poor or low-income conditions will tell you that they consider having healthy food and clean water as living the life of luxury because food and water are not freely made available everywhere to everyone.

Adequate shelter and clothing are also basic necessities that can be considered luxuries in stressed financial times. Although we know we all need protection from the climatic elements outside our homes, every person doesn't always have both. The cheapest way to get a house or new outfit is to make them, but making them requires proper tools, materials and skills.

Not every man can build a house from the ground up, and not every woman make clothes, shoes and jewelry. Furthermore, there are times when the breadwinners for the family are not able to afford to go and purchase the shelter and clothing either.

Education is also something that many cannot afford to pay for in a lump sum but need in every phase in life. Thankfully, like affection, education is also something that is free of monetary costs from time to time as long as a person shows commitment, promise and initiative. These *soft costs* (along with honesty, support and other things) are warranted by affection as well, yet money too is needed on occasions to remedy problems that only currency can cure. See, there is nothing that is totally free in this world. Everything costs something, even if nothing but time.

We all do what we have to do to get what we need to get. We have to accept that we must be willing to do or not do whatever we want to actually leave done or undone. And, since we all say we want the best and want to leave a good legacy, we all should know obtaining these things would never be free.

And why would we want it to be free since what *we think* is free we still don't appreciate (i.e., promo items, accusations, lies, etc.)? Maybe, because so much costs and we want relief from somewhere, anywhere? I know my ears perk up when I hear something is free too. But please, people. We have to stop allowing our willingness to see a certain thing take place be maimed by sayings that really do not ring truth but instead support idleness.

If we have to have sayings to go by, let's go by those that can be applied to our lives and remind us know our diligence can help us clear any hurdle in our path or make it up the steepest hills on windy days. Let's go by the sayings that show us new ways to solve old problems. Let's find liberation in sayings like, "Moving a mountain many times means making rocks crumble," and "You are the only sentient force in your life, so whatever continues in it is something you have approved."

Still, all the quotes in the world have no chance for creating a positive effect for a situation or society if those affected by the problem have other concerns that take priority. I guess, then, that what needs to be free is us of frailties including mistakenly believing things that sound good but are not true. Even better would be our freedom from our egos, wherein thereafter living is for experience and exchange rather than selfish conformity and outside validation. Freedom's been paid-in-full.

Literary & Visual Artist

Mylia Tiye Mal Jaza (aka Mary Michelle "Goddess Sage" Jefferson and Sun Child Wind Spirit) photographed and created the images – as well as wrote all the essays – included in **AND**. Released in December 2010 to offer solutions to a handful of the problems people face when trying to live a happy and peaceful life with others, the work serves to help readers accept their power of choice as the ultimate sign of their divinity and to empower themselves to make the world better by purposely making their own life better through choice and action.

The Mississippi native and former Uptown Dallas entrepreneur is currently a Chicago resident. She earned a bachelor's degree from Jackson State University in Jackson, MS, and a master's degree from the University of Texas at Dallas in Richardson, TX. She obtained an honorary doctorate from the Trinity Evangelical Christian University in Huntsville, AL, and is credited with nine other books to date.

Two of Mylia's books were works she republished that were written by ancestors of hers – The Facts Of Reconstruction by John R. Lynch and The Old Negro And The New Negro by T. Leroy Jefferson, M.D. The seven books she wrote prior to **AND** ranged in content from original poetry/prose and research to a novella and full-length film and television scripts. Those titles are: Life Is Beautiful: La Vita E Bella, Life Is Beautiful: La Vita Es Hermosa, Seen In Other Words, Plea For Peace, All For Show, Scientific Evidence God Exists, and Elegies of a Goddess.

An award-winning journalist / editor for newspapers and magazines, Mylia also operated an investment club that held shares of stocks including Google, Disney,

Microsoft and CVS. Additionally, she gives back to the community by cleaning

highways, feeding the homeless, providing school supplies to youth, and supplying Christmas gifts to nursing home residents. Mylia is also a noted vocalist who has performed at weddings, on recordings, during outdoor events, and onstage with Roz Allen, Karen Clark-Sheard, and Seven Benjamin. The business services she provides includes human resources, advertising, media relations, technical writing, web content, staff training, and book publishing.

(peoplewarmers.7p.com, bepublished.org)

www.ingramcontent.com/pod-product-compliance
Ingram Content Group UK Ltd.
Pitfield, Milton Keynes, MK11 3LW, UK
UKHW020216250726
13967UKWH00001B/20

9 780557 973187